MY

BLUE

EYES

MY BLUE EYES

Viewing the World Through an Atypical Lens

Joni J. Johnson, MD

ISBN: 9781728641065

This book is **dedicated** to so many people that I don't even know where to start . . .

I must first dedicate this book to my mother, **Gwendolyn W. Johnson**, who has always been my biggest fan. Without you and your relentless edits of every paper and project that I ever completed during my primary and secondary school years, I don't know that I would have ever graduated. You demonstrated hard work, ambition, strength, commitment, integrity and an unwavering love for your family. I am who I am because of you. Thanks! I Love You.

My father, **Ronald T. Johnson**, who will always live with me in spirit, taught me how to be self-sufficient and not to be dependent on anyone. Through your eyes I could accomplish anything, and I believe in myself because you first believed in me. I was inspired to create a legacy because of the legacy you left for me. I Miss You and will always Love You.

My brother, **Eric Johnson** aren't you glad I pulled you off the beach in California to reluctantly join my journey? You had no idea what you were getting into, but the best is yet to come. This book was your vision, not mine so I hope you got what you asked for. Thanks for your encouragement, support and commitment. I Love You.

My kids; **Robyn Peterson**, **Avery Johnson-Edmonds**, **Sydnee Johnson-Edmonds** and my grandson, **Jaxon Johnson**. Everything that I do is because of you. With all of my long hours, business trips, deployments and constant time on the computer, I have tried my best to be present for you. I am far from the best mom ever, but I try daily to be the best that I can be. Like this book, I am a work in progress and in need of frequent editing, but I appreciate your understanding. Thank you for loving me, my love for each of you is endless.

My staff, my patients and anyone and everyone that I have or will influence with my story—I tell my story because I want to inspire yours. Thank you for allowing me to be even a small part of your life. You keep me going and you make me better.

Finally, I must give all honor and praise to my God. I am who I am because of whose I am. This journey was not self-selected but God-directed. Once I surrendered to Your will, my purpose became clear. Thank You for selecting such a fulfilling purpose, this ride has been far from boring.

Table of Contents

Acknowledgments

This has been a labor of love in more ways than one. I would like to acknowledge my daughter, Robyn Peterson; my cousin, Dexter Roger Dixon; and my friend, Dr Tracy Harris who edited my first draft and provided invaluable feedback. Many props to the Self-Publishing School who provided a comprehensive framework for completing the production of this book from formal outlining through marketing. With their help the process of writing a book was not as intimidating as I first thought.

Special thanks to my Launch Team members who dedicated time from their very busy schedules to proofread the book and share my message with their friends via social media, radio and through private meetings. This book would not be what it is without your hard work and personal commitment.

Thanks for believing in me. You have no idea how much you are appreciated!

Latrice Claiborne, Launch Team Leader
Robyn Peterson, JD
Eric Johnson
Ronna McNair
David O. White, EdD
Torshau Cole Moore
Angela Trammel
Nichole Brathwaite-Dingle, MD
Tonya Touchstone, MD
D. Roger Dixon
LaTasha Blanton, DPT
Quintus McDonald
Lindsey Henry
Yolanda Reid, MD
Donna Gold
Takiyah Roberts Alexander
Sharon Pettway, MD

MY BLUE EYES

Viewing the World Through an Atypical Lens

It's funny to me that I'm writing a book because I'll never read it. I actually hate to read. That's right I said it—I hate to read. Your mouth just dropped didn't it? Here I am, an accomplished doctor and I hate to read. But, why is that something that causes people's mouths to drop? I assume it's because doctors are supposed to love to read, be inspired, and be motivated by the idea of being a lifetime learner? I can't believe I just typed that phrase either—lifetime learner. I remember the first time I heard that phrase in medical school. I thought, "Are you kidding me? I'm only signing up for 4 years of this. Am I really going to have to keep studying even after I get my degree?" It was the first hour of my medical school career and already I was considering leaving. It was the first time I thought about giving up my dreams, and it surely wasn't the last.

I digress.

Back to my love-hate relationship with reading. . .Reading for me hurts. Physically hurts. It started hurting in second grade and it hurts to this day. I can only read for a brief period before my eyes get heavy and a headache ensues. If I stop reading as soon as the symptoms start, I'm usually okay. Now that I think about it, my issues are probably more psychological than anything. I had visual therapy to correct my problem, but I think I suffer from PTSD (post-traumatic stress disorder) onset by the mere thought of having to read.

Another issue: I have dyslexia and a visual convergence insufficiency. Being dyslexic makes it difficult for me to understand what I'm reading, and the visual convergence affects how I process the words, letters, symbols, and shapes in space. Despite these issues, despite my complete and utter disdain for reading, I still buy books. That's the funny thing. If you go into my office, I have a shelf full of books. Books that, of course, I have never read. Here's another funny thing. I actually get excited about a book and what might be in it, it's just after the first page that I'm not excited anymore. To be completely honest, I think I like the idea of people thinking that I'm learned (whatever that means).

As I said earlier, second grade was when the hurt first started. I knew then that something wasn't right. I just didn't know it had a name or what that name was. I told my parents that I didn't like to read and that reading hurt. Being that they were educators, they didn't take me seriously. In fact, no one took me seriously. Not my parents, friends, or teachers.

In fourth grade, I finally convinced a teacher to listen. Little did I know she may have listened but didn't actually *hear* me. She allowed me to go to the Reading Resource room with the other kids who struggled to read, but not for the reasons she should have or the reasons I wanted her to. I think she saw the Reading Resource room as a reward for me. I was able to get out of the classroom and help the special education teacher with the kids who needed help. My grades never reflected a need for help. Who would suspect a child with basically straight A's throughout her entire primary and secondary education struggled immensely to read?

The point is: I didn't receive any help when I got to that Resource Room. The teacher would give me a book and tell me to sit in the corner while she helped the other kids. In retrospect, I now know that it's not supposed to work like that. As an educator, you don't ignore a child's cry for help, *no matter how small that cry is*. But back then, I didn't know what to think other than, "These teachers are as stupid as I am. Why give a kid who can't read a book and tell them to read to themselves? Like staring at the book is going to miraculously make the words and meaning come to me." I started shaking my head back then.

I know you're probably asking yourself why I'm even writing this book in the first place. To be honest, I ask myself the same question and the answer is complicated. Since I began my career as a Pediatrician in the United States Army, people have been telling me I need to write a book. After speaking with patients, groups and colleagues, they often comment about how this information needs to be available to readers. Maybe it's time I listened. Not to get too religious or spiritual, but I believe that God sends messages through other people. Because

I can't afford to block any blessings, it's time to take a leap of faith and start writing.

I'm not a writer. I think I made that perfectly clear. But in the spirit of going with God, I'm going to push through, regardless of my hesitations. Like with most things that I do, I'll figure it out as I go along. Hopefully I continue to capture your attention and you continue to embark on this journey with me. Hopefully I luck out and have an amazing product. Scratch that. Let me correct that statement, I don't luck out because I am probably the unluckiest person on the planet. However, I am most certainly *blessed*. So, I should say, I pray that God continues to speak through me and makes this work. I think that's a much more accurate statement. Gotta give Him His props, I surely wouldn't be where I am without Him.

Back to the book and its framework. My plan is to tell you all of my secrets. I'm going to tell you the good, the bad, and the ugly. Complete transparency. In addition to telling all of my own secrets, I plan to tell some of the secrets of my patients. Keep in mind: I'm a doctor. I have legal and ethical obligations to maintain the privacy and confidentiality of my patients. As such, I'm not going to use their names. Nor will I disclose any identifying information. Doing so would be a HIPPA violation. And quite frankly, I don't think an orange jumpsuit and manual labor is really how I want to spend the next 5-15 years of my life (orange really isn't my color).

Throughout the following pages, I hope to give you, as my reader, insight. No one is perfect. We all have our own obstacles to overcome to make this the best life that we have to live. My belief, which I share often, is that God made me with a few burdens to bear so that I will be able to help others like me to carry theirs as well. We all have a purpose and I'm so fortunate to have discovered mine. I want to help you discover yours. Hopefully, this book will help you take a close and deep look at yourself, embrace your flaws, fix those worth fixing, expel those not worth your time, and then move out of your own way to be a blessing to others.

I tell my patients' story because they are real, and they are raw. There's the old saying, misery loves company and the reality is that we all feel better when we are not alone. Some of you may relate to my experience and others may see yourselves or your children in my patient's experiences. I am always amazed after giving a presentation with a story about my patient Justin, how many people will say that they have a *Justin* at home. Sometimes you don't even recognize that there is an issue until you hear that someone else had the same experience that you just suffered through the night before. Finally, I have to be honest. I know some of you are like me and reading is really not your most favorite thing to do (hence why this book is less than 100 pages) and others may struggle with maintaining their attention. By adding a patient story at the end of each chapter, I intend to keep you interested and engaged. Let's hope it works.

As with all that I do, I'm about to let go and let God lead me on this journey of self-reflection and inspiration so that I can share some of the pearls that make me who I am and whose I am. Let's jump in!

Blue Eye Syndrome

Perspective is important. In my profession, we are taught to differentiate between normal and abnormal, typical and atypical. But is it really that easy? What do these terms actually mean? The typical response, more often than not, when a doctor says to a patient that something is abnormal or atypical, the patient hears something is wrong and needs to be fixed. In my personal and professional opinions, that's not always the case.

Before I present a lecture or workshop I believe that it is important for people to understand my perspective. I want people to know where I'm coming from, what my beliefs are, and, most importantly, my thoughts on this typical versus atypical phenomenon. I always frame my discussion around the Blue Eye Syndrome.

Take a moment and look in the mirror. Look into your eyes. What color are they? Brown? Green? Hazel? Blue? If you have blue eyes, then for the next few paragraphs I'll be speaking to you.

Here is the deal with blue eyes: blue is one of the least common eye colors worldwide. In fact, only eight percent (8%) of the world's population has blue eyes. If you are one of the select few blessed with blue eyes, as a physician I'm obligated to inform you that you have an Autosomal Recessive Trait. (I know that sounds scary, but we will get you through this). What does this mean? An autosomal recessive trait means that you had to get the blue eye gene from both of your parents. But it's not necessarily the dominant gene you inherited. I'm talking about the gene which may not be obvious in your parents. Simply put, if your parents have brown eyes, but you have blue eyes, they were carriers for the blue eye gene. Even if you don't see it in them, they gave it to you. I get it. This stuff is complicated, but also beside the point.

The point is, if you have blue eyes you are not typical. Given that only 8% of all people have blue eyes, you are very atypical. Being atypical may mean you can't see as well as the brown-eyed folks. Or it may mean you have difficulty finding outfits that match with your eyes. You may also be the only person in your class with blue eyes. People may look at you and stare because of your blue eyes. Your blue eyes can have a negative impact on your future. Why? Because you're different. You're atypical. You aren't like everyone else. Blue Eye Syndrome is a devastating diagnosis. Or is it?

The good news is you've known since birth you have blue eyes. Over the years you've grown, or learned, to appreciate those baby blues. You may have noticed how others appreciate your blues eyes as well. Sure, they may think you're atypical as you don't see too many people with eyes like yours. But they may also think your eyes are beautiful, alluring, hypnotizing even. That from birth you know that you have blue eyes and can learn to appreciate them. Your blue eyes may have gotten you several compliments and stares. As the days, weeks, and years go by, you realize your blue eyes, though different, aren't a barrier to your success. You eventually stop letting your atypical blue eyes be so. . .atypical.

To reiterate: having blue eyes is atypical (some may even say it's abnormal). But I see it differently. I see having blue eyes as being different but being different doesn't automatically mean that something's wrong and needs to be fixed. This perspective, my perspective, is the same vantage point that I use when working with my . patients who have Autism, ADHD and Learning Disabilities. My patients, and all others like them, don't need to be fixed. All they need is some TLC (Tender Lovin' Care), understanding, appreciation, and, most importantly, support.

CHAPTER 1:

In My Beginning . . .

Here's my story.

I was born the third, and last, child of Ronald and Gwendolyn Johnson. To be clear, I was the oops baby, which I was never able to forget. Apparently, I was conceived at a Kappa Alpha Psi Fraternity, Inc. convention in Chicago, Illinois. As the story goes, it appears that Mom was in graduate school at the time. On the day in question she was in the hotel room studying while Dad was partying with his frat in the ballroom. He came to the room for a quick *intermission* (if you catch my drift). Nine months later, I was born. Oops! Did I mention my parents were over 40 at the time? It seems as if too much partying and studying made for a realization that at age 40 and 45, respectively, Mom and Dad needed to get some things together. In any event, I always thought the story of my conception was too much information. I'm sure reading this, you feel my pain.

So why did I share? One, misery loves company. I've been victimized by this story for fifty years. Two, I find the ages of my parents to be extremely significant. At the time of my birth, my parents were getting serious. They were settled in their ways, and in their careers and they were about business. My mom was the stereotypical African American woman in the 60's. She worked hard to take care of her husband, kids, and household in an era of segregation. She dreamed of a career. The mere thought of slaving in a dead-end job inspired her to pursue her graduate degree. Gwendolyn Johnson, though the stereotypical embodiment of strength manifested in the form of an African American woman, was atypical. It wasn't typical for a woman, a black woman, in the 60's to have a graduate degree. It certainly wasn't typical for said woman to obtain a *second* graduate-level degree. But then there was my dad. Ronald, or Ronnie as my mom so affectionately called him, was highly educated as well. In fact, he graduated with his master's from Springfield University. Here's the issue, and ultimately the nexus of my own learning issues, if you let Mom tell it, she was the one who wrote most of his papers (to include his final thesis). My guess? Dad probably struggled academically, much like myself, but his learning disability went undiagnosed.

As the final child of significantly older parents, I like to think I was raised in a more mature fashion. Let me explain. My sister, who is my closest sibling in age, is four years older than I am. My brother, on the other hand, is fifteen years older. I actually didn't get to know my brother until much, much later in life. He was off to college by the time I was old enough to realize who he was. Because of the significant age differences, I was my sister's tag-a-long. I was able to hang out with the big kids. It helped that I matured faster than she did, so her friends often overlooked the fact that I was the younger sister.

Despite being the tag-a-long, by nature, I was quiet, reserved, and liked to spend time by myself. Looking back, I also preferred to be around older people like my sister's friends or adults. This was probably because those were the people I spent most of my time around. My parents were very social and did a lot of pop calling (if you know what pop calling is, you are really old school). Pop calling is when you just popped up at someone's house without calling first to hang out. There was always someone at my house or we were always at someone else's house. In retrospect, all the pop calling that we did growing up is why I can't stand people showing up unannounced to this day. But that was the culture back in the day, just don't try that with me now—trust me, I won't answer the door.

Despite the pop calling, the tag-a-longs and being well liked with a knack for making friends, I didn't like to be around a lot of people. I preferred more intimate settings where it was just me and one friend. To be honest, I only had one good friend at a time growing up and when that friend decided they wanted another best friend I would just move on to someone else. I also preferred boys over girls. Girls were always so petty, and I didn't have time for that. It was always drama and always seemed to revolve around a boy. I had more male friends than anything, but I didn't have many boyfriends. What I always found was odd was that when I did have a boyfriend, I constantly had to watch my back. There was always some girl who wanted to jump me because the boy she liked, liked me. REALLY?!? Who has time for that? I remember walking home from school one day with a bunch of girls following me saying they were going to jump me. I still find it funny that I would walk home, all by myself, with the gaggle of geese following me, and not once did anyone reach out and touch me. You would think they would have lost interest when they realized I didn't seem afraid like they wanted. I knew they were there (how could I not since they were yelling at me the entire way?), but I also knew I was not going to voluntarily stop walking. In my mind, they were my groupies and if they wanted to escort me home then I was going to let them. Why not?

I've always found a way to see a situation from a different perspective. This ability has allowed me to mentally endure and persevere. It also speaks to my mantra that "life is a game; winners figure out how to play that game better than anyone else." I've always seen myself as a winner.

Back to the girls. By the time I got home that day, I realized my dad knew that I was followed home. He decided to pick me up from school going forward. I want to emphasize that point—I didn't ask for a ride; he offered. I wasn't scared of those girls and they knew it. They had plenty of opportunities to fight me if they wanted to but chose not to take them. But let it be known: If they tried, I was a winner.

I was pretty self-confident on the outside growing up. That's right. On the **outside**. On the inside, I had some insecurities, but no one would ever know. In my household we were frequently told to fake it till you make it. No matter what, better hold your head up high at all times. Make them think you know what you are doing, even when you don't. To this day, I use that as my governing principle. (I thank God daily for the internet which makes it so much easier to fake it). It's funny but recently, my Administrative Assistant came in my office with a potential patient on hold who had asked if I knew about some obscure genetic condition which of course I had never heard of. I told her to hold that thought, went to Google, read the summary (because you should know by now I am not going to read the entire article) and then turned to her and said, "yes, I am familiar with that condition." Look, if you think that all doctors keep this stuff in their heads, you are delusional. There may be a few that remember this stuff but most of us turn to the internet like everybody else and yes, I learned how to do that in medical school.

By the time I was in middle school and high school I mastered the art of playing the game and faking it 'til you make it with respect to my education. I used my spare time to relearn the material taught in class instead of socializing with friends. I utilized my educator-parents as resources when I needed reinforcement. I also developed a system of reinforcement that involved Cliff Notes and books on tape. When that wasn't available, I used study groups or discussed the content with my mom so that I could learn the information through auditory means. I know now that I am an auditory learner, but back then I just knew that reading didn't work for me, so I needed to hear and not see what was important to get it.

This, my learning and retention difficulties and my choice to push through, developed my drive and determination.

Though I felt stupid at times, especially when I had to read something, I was not going to let anyone think I was stupid. I worked hard to prove to myself that I was smart. I worked really hard actually. I took Honors and AP classes. I graduated very close to the top of my class. Most importantly, I learned to defer gratification. I didn't have a whole lot of fun, but I kept telling myself the fun was going to come. Side note: I'm still waiting for the fun to come, but I'm almost there.

In my family, college was not an option, in fact it was considered an extension of high school and mandatory. I remember growing up and not being taught how to cook or clean the house like the rest of my friends (trust me, I'm wasn't complaining). My grandmother was a domestic with a high school education and one generation removed from slavery. My parents would say that they didn't want us to have domestic skills to fall back on, we had to do more with our lives so that we could offer more to our children. I dreamed of attending an Ivy League university and majoring in pre-med. I really didn't want to be a doctor for myself, but I wanted to be the doctor that my dad didn't have the opportunity to be. I knew it would take hard work but that was all I knew anyway. I didn't realize then that my mom had been my crutch and would not be going to college with me, but failure just wasn't an option. As with everything else to this point, I would figure it out. Little did I know that my expectations for college would take a huge turn to the left.

Don't Let My Intelligence Fool You

Johnny, a 4-year-old, was having difficulty in his daycare program. To be accurate, this was the second daycare program in the last 6 months that threatened to kick him out. His Dad came to clinic with concerns regarding Johnny's aggressive and disruptive behaviors. Dad stated that Johnny was always on the go, just like the energizer bunny, and would frequently get in trouble for screaming, hitting teachers, and throwing objects around the classroom. He was also very argumentative and argued with adults who he didn't acknowledge as authority figures. After much research, Johnny's parents felt that he may have attention deficit hyperactivity disorder (ADHD) and/or oppositional defiant disorder (ODD) and brought him in for evaluation to confirm their suspicions.

During the medical evaluation, Johnny was found to be very mature for his age, especially with regard to speech. He was able to answer all of the providers' questions with extreme detail. He was also much more interested in having a conversation with the provider than he was playing with the Matchbox cars that were provided to him. In fact, once Johnny lined up all the cars by size and color, he was no longer interested in them.

Dad stated that Johnny liked to have everything done his way. If he didn't get his way it would lead to destructive behavior and/or a temper tantrum. Johnny also interrupted adult conversations because he often felt that he had something to contribute to the conversation. Johnny enjoyed talking about many adult topics including history, politics, and natural disasters, which was his favorite. Johnny often got in trouble for talking when he was supposed to be quiet. He had difficulty sitting still, would run from his parents in parking lots and was easily distracted by about anything that was more exciting than the task at hand.

According to Johnny, he had a lot of friends. However, Dad added that he would only play with a peer whom Johnny felt to be his equal. Johnny had to be in control. He could be a reciprocal player with others, but he preferred parallel play.

Dad stated that after Johnny was removed from his first day-care program about 6 months ago prior to his clinical visit, they took him to the local Early Intervention program for evaluation. The evaluation concluded with a determination that Johnny's behaviors were normal and did not warrant further evaluation.

Johnny was evaluated by the team and found to have an intellectual quotient (IQ) in the superior range, ADHD, ODD and autism level 3. He was referred for speech therapy services for social language development, occupational therapy for sensory integration, and applied behavioral analysis (ABA) therapy for functional and adaptive interventions. Johnny was also enrolled in a social skills group to learn how to relate to same-age peers.

Johnny's high intellectual abilities made it easy for him to impress adults with his language skills and it didn't hurt that he was also a charming child. So charming, in fact, that his behaviors were excused by his first assessment team and essentially no interventions were recommended to assist his parents in supporting his needs. Don't let a child's intelligence fool you into believing that their behaviors are okay, and they don't need help.

CHAPTER 2:

The Long Grey Line . . . West Point (for real)

How does a kid with an unrecognized learning disability make it to West Pont? I think the real question is: Why would a person with an unrecognized learning disability WANT to go to West Point? The answer is I didn't! Can I tell you, I'm really beginning to feel like I have lived my entire life doing what other people have wanted me to do. Mind you, I've always used it to my advantage, but looking back on things, this is ridiculous. I digress. Here's the story.

I was sitting at the dining room table completing my college application for Northwestern University when my mother came home with this large envelope. At the time, she was a high school guidance counselor at John Adams High School in Cleveland, Ohio. Earlier that day, a recruiter who was trying to encourage more African Americans to apply for the United States Military Academy at West Point came to her school. Needless to say, she was impressed. So, impressed that she devised this plan to encourage me to apply during her fifteen-minute ride home. Let her tell the story, she needed to do research, a study, if you will. She claimed this would be an awesome opportunity for her students, but she needed to fully understand the process to better assist those students who were interested in attending. In hindsight, this was not part of her job description and part of me knew this. After all, that's what the recruiter was for. I will admit, I was a tad naïve.

Anyway, my mother drops this envelope on the table and tells me to fill it out. Of course, I wasn't interested. Joining the military NEVER crossed my mind. My initial thought was, who would want to do that? Not only that, but the application for West Point was nothing short of a novel. But, after looking at the application, and thinking long and hard, I made a deal with her. Since I had no intentions of EVER going to West Point, and she assured me that I would NEVER have to go, I suggested that she complete the application and I would sign it. I should have known that when she agreed without discussion or push-back that I was being set up.

The application was in and the next thing I know I get a letter saying that I need to take a physical exam. I didn't understand why my doctor's certification was not sufficient, but I figured why not, it's just a physical. Naïve doesn't begin to describe what I was; let's just call it oblivious. First, we had to drive almost an hour to get to the facility where the physicals were being conducted. Second, the physical, itself, took all day. Prior to that, never in my life had I been so thoroughly examined. I guess one good thing that came out of the experience was that they found a heart murmur I never knew existed. Bad part: I needed to have more tests.

As if the extremely intrusive physical wasn't enough, I was also required to have a Congressional endorsement to attend West Point. Luckily for me, I was a page for the Honorable Congressman Louis Stokes who was also a friend of my parents. Since I was going through the ringer simply so my mother could conduct research, I just knew my parents could handle this one. Easy. Nope, wrong again. I had to get dressed up and have an interview with the Congressman. I later discovered it was all just a formality, but it was time and stress nonetheless.

I was really starting to get annoyed by this process. All of this for some RESEARCH?! Then, on top of everything else, I received a call saying I needed to take a physical fitness test. WHAT?!? Ok, I was done—this was too much. I marched up to my mom and told her I was done. Further, I didn't have time for this; I wasn't going anyway. Think that worked? Nope! Before I knew it, I was out training with my dad, P.E. teacher and Athletic Coach Extraordinaire. Luckily, I was a Varsity Cheerleader and played Varsity Softball. I wasn't afraid of physical activity. But like I said, this was really getting old by now. Not to mention the fact that the skills stations made absolutely no sense to me. What is the point of a flexed arm hang anyway? (After over twenty years in the Army, I still don't know the answer).

Finally, I finished all the application requirements for West Point and I could get back to waiting for acceptances to the colleges that I really wanted to go to. My mind was already set that I was going pre-med at Northwestern or I was going to enter one of the six-year medical programs in Ohio. I just knew I was going to get in.

Then *it* happened. A large package arrived from the United States Military Academy (West Point). Inside was a large green padded folder with a formal letter of acceptance on one side and a very official looking, frameable certificate on the other side. Despite the amazing presentation, I was instantly overwhelmed with a feeling of doom. I knew it was over. I had never really had an opportunity in high school to be social, to go to parties and join fun clubs. I wanted college to be different. I wanted to be an AKA (Alpha Kappa Alpha Sorority, Inc.) like my mom and date a Kappa (Kappa Alpha Psi Fraternity) like my dad. I wanted to hang out in the student union and get an apartment off campus when I was a Junior. I had it all planned in my head and now all I could see were uniforms, crew cuts and rules. I considered myself a fashionista and always had the bomb hairstyle and now I would have to wear the same clothes as boys and look like a boy, every day. Yikes! I looked to my parents and they had the biggest smiles plastered on their faces accompanied with the scariest look of pride that I had ever seen them display. And then they said it, almost in unison, YOU GOT IN!!!! I was done, all I could do was try to down play this moment. I realized that it was an honor to be accepted to West Point and that very few people make it through the rigorous process and meet all of the qualifications and then actually get accepted. I realized I was one of the elite few, but. . .I really, really didn't want to go.

So, in a very smug and immature adolescent way, I said "I'm glad the research is done, I hope you now have everything you need to help your students get into West Point." Why did I think it would end there? They asked why I didn't want to go. Why would I want to go, I didn't know anyone at West Point or in the military? I saw myself chilling in the student union at a real college and joining a sorority, not wearing a uniform and marching. Next thing I know, I'm having an out of body experience and actually signing my name on the acceptance card. I was told that it would just sit on the dining room table while I thought long and hard about whether I wanted to go to a school that was equal in education to an Ivy League and was FREE. More importantly if I went and didn't like it I could leave after two years without obligation and transfer to Northwestern. Sounded good but I knew there was a catch. So, I agreed to let the card sit on the dining room table while I thought about it. I don't know why I was surprised when the next day the card miraculously disappeared off the table and the following week I received a letter about their upcoming freshman orientation. Duped again!

Normalized

Kyle was a 3-year-old male who had been referred to a local speech therapy practice for evaluation of a potential speech delay. While there, the Speech Therapist mentioned to Mom that during their evaluation, Kyle exhibited behaviors that could be consistent with autism and they recommended that Mom seek further evaluation. Kyle's Mom met with me to discuss her concerns for Kyle. From the onset, Mom stated that she did not believe that Kyle had autism and she felt that the limited amount of the time that the speech therapist spent with Kyle was not sufficient enough for him to make the claims that he had. This was concerning to me because in my experience, this particular speech therapy practice is very knowledgeable of Autism and a large percentage of their practice is patients with Autism. Additionally, I have not known them to refer or even speak to a parent about Autism if they didn't have a high index of suspicion that the individual was autistic. I knew that I would have to really ask about even the subtle symptoms of autism to make sure that I didn't miss something.

Prior to the visit I had reviewed the 13-page Medical Summary that Mom had completed regarding Kyle's history from prenatal to present. I spent 30 minutes asking Mom all the pertinent questions and paid attention to not only her answers but her body language. Mom had me convinced that Kyle was not at risk for autism and I was on the fence as to whether we should move forward with a full-evaluation at that time. Until Mom mentioned her daughter. Now, this was not her daughter's appointment, but Mom thought that since she was here she would ask some questions to help her determine if her daughter needed an evaluation. Sally was a 10-year-old female who was really struggling socially in 5th grade. She didn't have many if any friends and her self-esteem was dropping quickly. Mom was concerned that Sally was depressed. She told me of a situation on the school bus where Sally had been bullied by some of the girls and this situation made Sally question if she fit in with her peers in school.

Mom went on to say that she was a nurse and sees a lot of herself in Sally. Mom stated that growing up she didn't really feel that she fit in but has learned over the years to compensate. She stated that she doesn't really like to socialize at work but as a nurse it is expected so she will force herself to talk to the other nurses and participate in activities like everyone else. When she gets home from work though she is exhausted from the energy she must expend to be social and will retreat to her room to be by herself for the rest of the night. Mom said that as a family, they really don't interact with each other much. They all, meaning her husband, daughter and son, prefer to be alone. Mom then said, maybe she doesn't see there is an issue with her son or daughter because they are so similar in personality to her and her husband. Maybe, people outside of her immediate family can see things that she cannot.

Based on Mom's insight (or lack thereof), we decided to evaluate both children for neurodevelopmental issues like ADHD and autism, learning issues and mood disorders. Not surprisingly, we found that both children had autism and Sally's autism had her into a depression as well. We also discovered that both parents also have autism.

Autism had been normalized in this family so much so that they didn't see social issues that their children were having as problems but instead they felt that their social relationships were to be expected. With understanding and supportive therapy this family gained a new perspective on how to approach uncomfortable social situations.

CHAPTER 3:

Women at West Point . . . Let the Games Begin

So, the plan as my parents explained it to me was that I would go to West Point for 2 years, quit without owing any obligation to the military and then transfer all of my credits to Northwestern (where I had been accepted with a partial scholarship) and finish my college career in 3 years then off to medical school. It was a win-win, so they said. I would have an outstanding education and finish undergrad in 3 years instead of 4 and they would only have to pay for one year of college. Sounded good, right? It made a lot of practical sense, but these were my parents I was dealing with, they were crafty and always had something up their sleeve. . .I knew something was going to go wrong, I just didn't know what it was, but it didn't matter at this point. I was committed (literally—mentally and physically) so I was going to follow through.

Now, let's not forget my mantra that life is a game so there was no way I was going to go to West Point unprepared. I began to study my situation and read up on what this military life was all about. I was not thrilled with what I discovered. First there were uniforms—back in the day I was a real fashionista and the thought of wearing a uniform every day and a drab grey and black one that was wool and itchy was not appealing in the least. Next, the hair. Everybody had a crew cut, including the women! Previously, my hair was always on point; bobbed, asymmetric, whatever the current style was, and I was about to go someplace where a barber (not a beautician) was going to cut my hair. This was not going to be pretty. Also, I was not natural at the time, where was I going to get my relaxers? Barbers don't know how to work with chemicals. As I continued my research I learned about 23 credit hours per semester academically and a requirement to do drill and ceremony and participate in a sport or intramural activity—I was beginning to wonder if cadets at West Point were also given more than 24 hours in a day because I couldn't see how all of this was even possible. Then I heard about the plebes (freshman) having to ping (that means walking briskly like speed walking, whenever in a common area) and being hazed by upper classman on a daily for the entire freshman year. Times have changed now for cadets, but it was brutal when I was there.

The bottom line was, I really didn't like what I was learning. To make matters worse, I had declined all of the other college acceptances that I had received so there really was no turning back at this point.

I decided to take matters into my own hands. There wasn't much that I could do about the uniforms, so I gave all my cool clothes to my sister and let that one go. I decided to have my hair stylist cut my hair before I arrived at West Point so at least I could avoid the buzz cut from the barber. My mother was given the job of finding someone at West Point who could relax my hair and I have to say she came through with that one. She actually found a wonderful older lady who worked on the janitorial staff. She lived in Newburg (right outside the gate) and once every two weeks she would sneak me off post to her house and I would get my hair done and spend some quality time with her family. Back in the day, plebes couldn't regularly leave post during the first semester, so you had to get creative. I also joined the Gospel Choir which allowed me the opportunity to interact with upper classman (which plebes were also not allowed to do unless you were in a club or on a sports team) and traveled off post frequently. The Cadet Gospel Choir had trips around the United States at least once a month and we had rehearsal once a week, so I developed a strong support system and of friends and upperclassman who really taught me how to survive that first year.

The next hurdle to clear was the pinging and the hazing. Back in the day, the hazing was brutal (I think I said that already). It was all part of the military abasement process where they break an individual down and then build them up with the character and values that support a military way of life. I really wasn't feeling that concept, I mean it made sense in some respects but the idea of someone up in my face daily, yelling at me and making me do stupid stuff really wasn't what I was interested in doing. As always when I'm faced with a situation that I can't figure out a solution, God comes through. In this case, he paired me with a roommate named Carol Johnson. Now Carol was a blessing in many ways but the first was the most obvious—we shared a last name. Did I mention that Carol was also African American? Now the Corps was not made up of many African Americans at this time. I think they took in around 10%, which in a Corps of 3000 that made for about 300 African American students per year group. There were even fewer African American women. If my memory serves me correctly, I think we started our plebe year with a total of 9 African American females. We were divided into 36 companies across the Corps so really what were the chances of two being in any one company and being roommates? Exactly my point—this was divine intervention.

Now Carol was cool. She was much taller than I was, and she was a basketball player. We quickly became known as Johnson & Johnson, like the baby products; and she was big Johnson and I was little Johnson. We went everywhere together because we quickly realized that there was strength in numbers. As we would ping across the yard (let's not forget that she was significantly taller, so I had to ping twice as fast to keep up with her long legs), the upperclassman would yell out to us—"there goes Johnson & Johnson." When we would get hazed, it always seemed to be about baby products or something silly and almost never about cadet knowledge of the day. We were a big joke, which was okay with me. Most of the time, we didn't' even get stopped because the upperclassman thought we were so funny.

I was pretty proud of myself during my first year at West Point, because I had figured out how to tackle most of the obstacles and turn them to my advantage. Drill and ceremony was a challenge though because I would pass out frequently. We had to drill a couple times per week after classes and it was long, boring and hot. Anatomically, I have knees that hyperextend so even though they tell you not to lock your knees I couldn't help it and the blood would flow away from my brain and I'd go down—again. I had had enough of hitting the ground during drill, so I decided to try out for the Cheerleading squad instead. I made the team and so instead of going to drill, I would go to cheerleading practice after class and although I continued to hit the ground it only occurred when my partner, Eric, dropped me from a stunt.

I survived my first year of West Point and luckily, I had taken Advanced Placement and Honors classes in High School so academically I didn't struggle. The second year, academics became a real challenge. I could no longer rely on the fact that I had seen the material previously and the science and military history courses were really getting hard. The volume of reading increased tremendously, and I couldn't keep up. It was this year that I decided that pre-med at West Point was not an option. I settled into a Mechanical Engineering Management major (since in those days everyone at West Point had to take an engineering track) and medicine became a distant memory. I had to get creative and I remember devising a plan to succeed academically. I remember identifying classmates in each course who seemed to really understand the material and reached out to them to set up study groups. We would meet and talk about our assignments and the books we had to read to make sure that we understood the concepts and the assignments. Little did they know that I had not really read all of the assignments, I mean I tried, but it just never made sense to me until we talked it through. I didn't realize it then, but I was compensating for my undiagnosed learning disability. What I called it then was just survival. I just needed to endure this last year and play the game because I still had hopes of transferring to Northwestern to complete my college experience. Hope that would shortly be dashed . . .

As I was so focused on having a successful second year at West Point and earning credits that would transfer to another college or university, my parents were hard at work back at home. I didn't realize it at the time, but they were becoming invested in support of the United States Military Academy. They had become active members of the parent support group in Ohio and were attending meetings and avidly supporting the recruitment of new cadets. My mom, who had taught me to be fashionable, had changed up her wardrobe to include West Point trinkets like black, grey and gold hat and scarf sets and my dad was wearing West Point jackets and baseball caps. When they attended the Army Navy game that year to watch me cheer they came decked out with West Point pom poms and seat cushions. I should have known something was up just seeing my mom at the game since she never attended a game in all my years of being on my high school cheer team. And now, she was here, screaming for Army football wearing West Point garb? Writing this now, I don't know how I missed it; something was up but I really didn't notice until I went home over the Christmas break and then I saw it. On the bumper of both of my parent's cars, a place that had never before seen anything but an occasional scratch or dent from my mother hitting a trash can when backing out of the driveway, there it was. . .an "I Love My Cadet" bumper sticker. I remember thinking when I first saw it that it looked so permanent. Why would they affix that to their cars when they knew I had every intention of leaving West Point at the end of the year? Come to find out, it was no mistake. But don't forget, my parents are good. They didn't stop there. When I returned home at spring break to discuss submitting my applications to Northwestern I was greeted by an article in the Congressional Record where my congressman had submitted an update on my performance at West Point and how proud he was of me. Additionally, he was having an event that week and had invited me to attend and wear my uniform. The writing was on the wall, but I still chose to ignore it.

Finally, the end of the year came, and all second-year cadets were faced with the decision to declare that we would continue our education at West Point or elect to leave without obligation. I called my parents to notify them that I was not going to continue, and the first thing my dad said was, I guess I'll have to get a new car because I'll never get the "I love my Cadet" bumper sticker off.

I don't know why it was so hard for me to disappoint my parents, other kids do it all the time, but I just couldn't. So, I stayed. I had already figured out the ins and outs of West Point and I was doing well. I was a Rabble Rouser (cheerleader), my grades were good, I had established study groups, and I had awesome friends. I was also an upper classman which meant the hard part was over, I was the one doing the hazing now instead of receiving it. It wouldn't be that hard, and it wasn't. By senior year, I had bought a car and even though cadet parking was over a mile away from the dorm and we had curfew, I was still in town as much as possible. I hate to admit it, but by my last year, I actually starting recruiting for West Point and had wonderful experiences to share.

May 31, 1990, I graduated in the 10th year anniversary class of women at West Point and entered the Medical Service Corps as a Second Lieutenant.

What Happens When Your Compensatory Mechanism Fails

Jasmine was a 17-year-old athlete whose dream is to play soccer on the collegiate level. Her mom came to clinic for a consultation to discuss medications for ADHD. According to Mom, Jasmine was diagnosed with Attention Deficit Hyperactivity Disorder, Predominantly Inattention Type when in elementary school. At that time, it was recommended that Jasmine start a stimulant medication, but her parents were afraid of the long-term effects. Instead, they elected to put Jasmine in a tutoring program and Mom assisted her with her homework. Now that Jasmine was a senior in high school, Mom realized that she has probably been helping Jasmine a little too much.

Jasmine always had difficulty in school. She struggled to focus and to stay on task. Homework takes forever, partly because Mom had to re-teach Jasmine basic facts and information that she had learned in school but forgotten. Mom felt like she was constantly re-teaching Jasmine the same facts over and over. Once they got through the arduous task of getting through homework, Jasmine would forget to turn in the assignment which lowered her grade even more. Jasmine was also a horrible test taker and struggled to concentrate once everyone else finished their test and started moving around. She was always the last to finish. Even with tutoring and all the extra assistance Jasmine got from her parents, her grade point average is barely a 2.5. She was an awesome soccer player but concerned that with her grades and SAT scores she may not get accepted into her college of choice. Mom's biggest concern was not that she wouldn't get accepted but that she wouldn't have the focus of the discipline to be successful in college. Mom realized that she should have put Jasmine on medication sooner, in order to boost her confidence and make her less reliant on her Mom.

Prior to completing the assessment with our team, Jasmine received notification that she was not accepted to her college of choice. She obviously didn't take the news very well, but she was later called by the soccer coach who stated that he really wanted her to play for his team, so he would make sure she got in. Jasmine felt even more pressure to be able to succeed academically as well as athletically once she started college and really wanted medication as soon as possible.

Jasmine completed a comprehensive assessment with our team and was found to have an average intellectual quotient (IQ), ADHD-combined type and a specific learning disability in reading. She was started on a stimulant medication which helped with her focus and attention but there were so many holes in her knowledge base that she also needed to work with a reading specialist and her teachers to reinforce her knowledge. She also started behavioral therapy to learn organizational strategies to help manage her time between sports and academics.

When it was determined that Mom wasn't going to go to college with Jasmine, it was time to discover other ways to compensate so that she could succeed on and off the field.

CHAPTER 4:

So, This is What Failure Feels Like

Like so many cadets do, I got married right after graduation and spent my "honeymoon" in Panama where my then husband was assigned. I left after about a month to attend the Army Medical Department Officer Basic Course in San Antonio, Texas prior to arriving at Fort Lewis, Washington for my first duty assignment as an Army officer. My head was spinning, I didn't even know how I had made it this far, but I was on a roll. I had successfully completed my education at the United States Military Academy and had graduated with more than a 3.0 grade point average. I had been one of 4 cadets that had been selected into the competitive Medical Service Corps branch and had matched for my number one duty location which was Hawaii. That had to change when my husband was selected to train as a West Point math professor and the University of Hawaii did not have a graduate program in Math. Fort

Lewis was the next best assignment for both of us. I started my military career as an Ambulance Platoon Leader and did very well. From there I became a Treatment Platoon Leader and then went on to become an Adjutant/Personnel Officer for a Medical Evacuation Brigade. Life was great, but I still yearned to be a doctor.

Let's break down that desire to be a doctor a little bit. What I have realized as I have gotten older is that when you are young you do things for all kinds of reasons. As I look back, I have done much in my life not because it was something that I really wanted to do but I have convinced myself that I wanted to do it. I've spent a lot of time over the years really thinking about how these previous experiences have positioned me for my purpose and I am now convinced that God has been in the mix from the start and luckily for me I have been willing to go along (even if at times begrudgingly).

I digress again. . .being a doctor was really my dad's dream, not his dream for me but his dream for himself. He grew up during a time when it was hard for African Americans to become doctors, so he did what was the next best thing for him which was to study the human body as a physical education teacher. He frequently talked to me about his anatomy classes and his study of kinesiology and his dream that he couldn't make come true. I think the more we talked about it the more it became my desire for myself because I wanted it for him. I guess when you think about it, that may be how dreams develop. You learn about something to the point that you are inspired to learn even more and to become a part of it. I never really thought about it that way until just now, in the past I always saw my going into medicine as doing something for my dad but in reality, I think I have done it for myself but my passion for it was ignited by my dad and by my desire to give life to his dreams as well as my own. In any event, although I was happy and content to fulfill my military obligation as a Medical Service Corps officer, I just couldn't seem to let *our* dream die. Once again, God stepped in and provided another divine intervention.

One of my mentors in my unit mentioned to me about the Health Professions Scholarship Program (HPSP) where the military would provide funding for individuals to attend medical school. My husband would be assigned to West Point that coming fall to teach in the math department and I had just enough time to take the MCAT (medical school entrance exam) and apply for admission for medical school and the scholarship. I applied to all the medical colleges in New York that were within two hours of West Point and I only got accepted to two, New York Medical College in Valhalla and Albert Einstein College of Medicine in the Bronx. I received the HPSP scholarship to attend either college but although Valhalla was closer to West Point, I elected to go to the Bronx and Albert Einstein. I have frequently said in the past, and I will repeat it again; had I not attended Albert Einstein College of Medicine, I would not be a doctor today!

A Tale of Two Cities by Charles Dickens opens with "It was the best of times, it was the worst of times. . ." and that was how I began my medical career. Medical school is hard!! I think most people recognize that it can be challenging which is why everybody doesn't do it, but for me it was one of the hardest things I have ever done. Now, I am the first to say that nothing that I do is easy. I can make picking up groceries hard; everyone else will run to the store, find what they want, check out and come home. Not me. I'll go to the store and they won't have what I need, then I'll go to the next store and they still won't have it. By the fifth store they'll have exactly what I want but I won't be able to buy it because my credit card won't work. I'll go to get cash and by the time I get back to the store someone else will have purchased what I need. You get the picture, that's my life. So that's kind of how medical school was.

When I started medical school, my daughter, Robyn, was only six months old. Her father insisted that we have two separate households, he and Robyn lived at West Point and I had a studio apartment in the Bronx on campus. Ideally, I was supposed to focus on my studying during the week and go home to West Point and have family time on the weekend. Sounded good but it didn't really work out too well. First off, medical school is one of those programs where you are expected to study 24-7, like there are no weekends off. Also, as a new mother, it was very hard to be away from my child and really focus. Also, as a first-time dad in a new job, he wasn't that great on juggling a young infant, working and keeping the house together so much of my weekend was spent cleaning the house, doing laundry, grocery shopping, etc.

Now let's talk about the academic challenges. At this point, my learning disability was still undiagnosed so imagine a girl who has never been hooked on phonics trying to sound out sphygmomanometer. There are words in some of the medical books that I can't pronounce to this day. All of my compensatory mechanisms that I had developed also didn't work. Cliff doesn't make any notes for medical literature; study groups were held mostly on weekends when I wasn't there, and I didn't realize just how competitive medical school can be. Everybody was grinding, and no one was really interested in helping the next person get ahead. It was a perfect storm for failure.

Don't get me wrong, I put in the time. I sat for hours reading and re-reading the same passage wondering what it was saying. I stayed up late trying to prepare so that when I sat in the lectures I fell asleep because I was clueless and tired. My bed eventually became my friend and it just became easier to stay in bed and harder to get up. My only motivation my first year of medical school was the hot bagel from the "bagel man" food truck that sat in front of the lecture hall. I had to get a bagel every morning, so I figured I might as well go to class and listen to the lecture while I ate my bagel.

I found that I did well in classes that were interactive but classes that were visual were impossible. Histology class, which is a study of the microscopic structure of tissues, was the worst. All the tissues looked like blue and red dots to me and I couldn't understand how I was supposed to tell the difference between one tissue and the other. Needless to say, I failed that class miserably. Then came anatomy; now I loved anatomy. The dissections were cool, and the class was hands on. We worked in teams and we discussed all of the different parts of the body with our classmates and professors. I even went to extra anatomy labs just to make sure I understood everything. Mind you, I had to redeem myself after the disastrous Histology performance. When the final exam rolled around I knew I had this. I had even thought for a fleeting moment that I should consider surgery as a specialty.

The exam was held in the anatomy lab were the professor had tagged different parts of the cadaver and you had to say what organ, muscles, artery, vein, etc. the tag represented. But there was a catch that I was not aware of, they had removed the structure from the natural part of the body so that you didn't have any natural associations to rely on in determining the structure that was labeled. So, for example, they took the heart out of the chest, flipped it upside down, laid it on its side, put it on the cadaver's leg and attached the label to a tiny vessel that you had to identify. I was screwed! Without the natural associations, I had a hard time even knowing that I was looking at the heart. I failed anatomy, too. And for me in that moment, life just got real.

I had struggled to succeed my entire life, but I had succeeded. I had obstacles where there shouldn't even be an obstacle, but I always scaled them. Now I was faced with a heart—knee transplant and I had no clue what I was looking at and I was done. Or at least I thought I was done, but Albert Einstein was not done with me yet. Thank, God.

At the end of my first year of medical school, my marriage was a mess and I was preparing myself to return to the Army since I fully expected to be kicked out of the program. I went to the Student Services Office to find out the process for leaving school and transitioning back in to the Army when they asked me if I was planning on quitting school since they had no intentions of kicking me out. I was dumbfounded. I didn't think it was possible to fail not one but two courses in medical school and still expect to continue. Not only that, what residency program would ever accept me after seeing that I had failed two courses? To this day, it is hard for me to believe what happened next. I was told first and foremost, that I was accepted into medical school because they believed that I could do it. So long as I still wanted to be there, our next goal was to understand why I was struggling to succeed. I was also told not to worry about my transcript because I would repeat those two courses and so long as I passed that would be the only grade reflected on my official transcript that would be sent to residency programs. The only way anyone would know that I failed would be if I told them (I guess the cat's out the bag now).

Over the next month, the folks in student services arranged for me to have private cognitive educational testing done to determine what was interfering with my ability to read and comprehend. Once the first round of testing was completed, I went to another provider to confirm the findings of the first. They both confirmed that I have dyslexia (a learning disability in reading comprehension) and a visual convergence insufficiency. I was assigned a tutor for histology and anatomy and re-enrolled in both courses. I was referred to a Psychiatrist where I was diagnosed with major depression and started on medication and behavioral therapy. Lastly, I was given the opportunity to decelerate my academic schedule from a 4-year program to a 5-year program, I was provided extra time and a private room for testing and I was encouraged to only study during the week and spend the weekends with my family.

I would not be a doctor today if it weren't for Albert Einstein College of Medicine and a lot of divine intervention.

I didn't realize it at the time, but I had just been exposed to a framework for identifying a girl who cannot read and providing her with the tools to become successful. The framework I would eventually employ when working with struggling kids and adults in my multi-disciplinary private practice. For me, failure was an opportunity to develop the tools needed for long-term success . . .

A Different Perspective of Failure

Ray was a 13-year-old, 8th grader who came to see me because his grades had been falling and his parents were growing increasingly concerned. Ray had always been a high achiever and would even sacrifice spending time with other kids to study or do additional school work. This year was different. He appeared to be struggling to focus and stay on task and he was starting to outright refuse to do certain assignments in class and for homework. He felt more and more that he didn't fit in with the other kids and had a hard time making and keeping friends. This had always been the case, but middle school made it worse. Mom was fearing that he was getting depressed and at times he would even refuse to go to school.

Ray was evaluated by the team and was found to have a very high intellectual quotient (IQ), attention deficit hyperactivity disorder (ADHD), combined type and autism, level 1. When Ray was informed of the diagnoses he was thrilled because he now had a reason for feeling and thinking the way that he did. When he arrived home that day, Ray read everything that he could find on the internet about ADHD and autism and he saw so many similarities between himself and the information. He understood that because of his autism if he could reach the same conclusion he would push back against doing certain assignments that required him to use a method that didn't make sense to him or appeared to be more labor intensive. He had always been uncomfortable spending too much time with friends or other people and preferred to be by himself. He didn't really understand why his sister enjoyed being with others and it was really annoying to him. After researching, he understood that many people with autism are socially awkward and prefer to be alone. He was relieved to learn that ADHD makes focusing on a non-preferred task hard and sometime people with ADHD need help to stay on task or to not get distracted by things around them or even the thoughts in their head. All of this reassured Ray that he was okay and that there were reasons why his grades were dropping. Ray asked to be started on medication because he wanted every advantage to succeed in school.

When Ray returned to clinic for his medication follow-up appointment, he appeared much happier and content with his performance in school. He stated that the medication was working well, and he didn't have any concerns. His dad didn't see things the same way that Ray did. Ray's dad was not happy about the diagnosis of autism and didn't agree that he exhibited the characteristics. More importantly, his dad felt that by giving Ray the diagnoses of ADHD and autism, he had been given an excuse to fail. This perspective didn't make sense to me because according to Ray, he was doing much better in school and was performing to his high standards. When I asked Ray, what his dad was referring to he didn't seem to understand either.

I then asked Ray's father to tell me what he meant when he stated that Ray had been given an excuse to fail. He responded by stating that Ray had received an F in his Latin class. Upon hearing this, I asked Ray to tell me about Latin; isn't Latin an elective class. Ray stated that Latin is an elective and he wanted to take the class because he thought it would be fun and would help him in some of his other classes. What he discovered was that not only was it not fun, but it also didn't make any of his other classes easier. At that point he needed to make a decision. He went to his counselor to take a hard look at his schedule. Since he was in his last year of middle school he realized that these grades would not be reflected on his transcript for college. He had also intended to take a foreign language to have more room in high school for another elective which meant that he could still switch to another foreign language next year and still have enough credits for an advanced diploma. Lastly, his grades were A's and B's in all his other classes, so an F in Latin would not seriously hurt his grade point average. Armed with all of this information, Ray made the conscious decision to not put any more effort into Latin and instead put all of his effort into his other classes.

After listening to the explanation, I asked Ray's dad if he understood his reasoning. His dad responded that Ray had never explained it to him that way. Ray's response was, "he never asked."

In essence, from Ray's perspective he did not fail Latin instead he chose not to pass. One of the gifts of autism, is being able to view the world from a totally different lens.

CHAPTER 5

Exceeding the Scope of Practice

Residency at Children's Hospital of Michigan is somewhat of a blur right now. I remember spending many long nights and days with little to no sleep (this was before the residency restriction on the number of post-call working hours). I remember spending several weeks in Senegal, West Africa doing developmental research with one of my "Senegal Sisters" and I remember graduating a month after my peers because I needed extra time to study and pass the USMLE Step 3 exam to obtain my licensure. I had hoped when I finished medical school that my academic struggles were behind me, but I quickly realized that to be a lifetime learner it could continue to plague me. I realized quickly that my strength was the personal interactions that I shared with my patients. I would build on that strength going forward and allow it to overshadow my weaknesses and the fact that I couldn't seem to retain anything that I wasn't exposed to on a daily basis.

I remember being very anxious starting my first real job as a Pediatrician. I was assigned to Darnall Army Community Hospital in Fort Hood, Texas. Typically, all new staff pediatricians start in July because you finish your residency program in May or June and then have several weeks to move and get settled. As I mentioned earlier I was about a month behind this process, so I didn't get there until August. Can I tell you being anxious doesn't really describe how I was feeling? Fort Hood is the largest Army installation in the United States and it houses two full Army Divisions which means it also is the home to a tremendous amount of well and sick kids. This meant I really needed to be on my game. I was also rejoining the Army after an 8-year break in service, so I felt that I was relearning how to be a soldier. Lastly, since I didn't attend the military medical school or a military residency I wasn't part of the club and didn't understand the intricacies of military medicine. I also wasn't as comfortable then as I am now with my academic shortcomings. I was embarrassed that I struggled with test taking and hadn't easily passed my licensing exams like I felt EVERYBODY else had. I prayed no one would ask me why I was starting my career later than the rest.

The good news was that being in the military is like riding a bike as they say. Once the uniform was back on it was like I had never been without it and honestly not much had changed. We still saluted with the right hand and enlisted soldiers were still the heart of the Army. Leadership and responsibility were still an essential part of running any organization and a military hospital was no different than a field unit. Rank still had its privileges and responsibilities so even though I was late to the party, because of my prior service I out-ranked most of my peers and quickly found myself with several additional duties and positions of authority that really had nothing to do with my clinical fund of knowledge.

The other good news was that no one expected me to have all pediatric medicine memorized. They expect that for the written tests that you must take but I guess they realized that real life is something very different from a test.

I must digress for a moment to mention something that was very important to my military journey during my first year as a Staff Pediatrician. I failed to share earlier that I completed my residency in 2001 which meant that I arrived at Fort Hood in August of 2001. After only being there about a month, I believe it was my second call as a newly trained, full-fledged doctor and the date was September 11, 2001. Now call at Fort Hood was no picnic in the park. When you were on call you were humping. If you were lucky you had a resident with you but if you weren't (and of course luck does not run in my bloodstream) you were covering the Emergency Room, Pediatric Ward, Newborn Nursery, Neonatal Intensive Care Unit (NICU) and newborn deliveries all by yourself. Prior to starting call you also work most of the day in the clinic seeing patients and then about 1600 military time (4:00 pm) your shift begins. If you remember what you were doing on September 11th as most of us do, there was a lot of chaos in the beginning. We were all crowded around the television at first then there was the mass exodus of people wanting to get home to make sure they were with their families and everyone was safe. At this point, we had no idea that this was a terror attack, so all my colleagues went home and before long it was just me in the hospital representing Pediatrics along with the other on-call representatives from their clinical services and the night shift of nurses and ER physicians. Early on, we all checked with friends and relatives that we had in New York and I learned that my husband's cousin and one of my best friend's husband had both been at the World Trade Center and were both unaccounted for. Pretty quickly as the story started to develop and as we became more aware that this was terrorist activity, the world shut down. The military installations closed to all incoming and outgoing traffic, the airspace was shut down and we were limited on our cell phone use. It seemed that the only contact I had with the outside world was what I could learn from the news. I did get word that my husband's cousin was safe and hadn't quite made it to work when the event happened, but my friend's husband was still missing. Then my shift really began . . .

I received a call to come to the Emergency Room for a 9-month old infant who just made it in before the installation locked down. He had been left in the care of his mother's boyfriend during the day who was not having a good day either. The story was that the boyfriend had just made some noodles and placed them on the coffee table and the infant knocked them over and was burned. Seemed reasonable, until you saw the baby. This baby was burned over 30 percent of his body and they were not splatter burns but submersion burns. This was clearly abuse. I believe I mentioned earlier that this was only my second call as a solo Pediatrician and in light of the fact that this was September 11th the word solo really took on new meaning. Typically, when there are abuse cases there are individuals who assist the doctor to obtain information and interview the parents or guardians. Those individuals were not in the hospital that evening. Typically, an individual with 2nd and 3rd degree burns are initially stabilized by the surgeons and then transported to the Burn Center in San Antonio for continued care. The surgeon was taking home call (translation they were not in the hospital either) and the airspace was closed even to medical evacuation due to the terror attack. It was just me (because once the ER doctor consults a specialist it became my case) and I had never managed a severe burn case before. This was the day that I realized that books were in fact my friend and I really understood how medicine works. Although I felt very much alone, I had the surgeon who helped me to manage the baby's replacement fluids via the phone and everything else I needed to know I found in one of my medical references. I had been so anxious thinking that a good doctor knows everything off the top of her head and is expected to react immediately with a plan of action.

That day I realized that a good doctor is always surrounded by a good team and the best doctor knows what she does not know and is willing to admit to the patient that she doesn't know and must consult the references. I know this seems simplistic, but you would be surprised that some doctors feel that they can't admit to not knowing something and instead will resort to going with what they do know even if it isn't the best solution for the patient. Now don't get me wrong, I'm not throwing shade on the medical profession or on my colleagues

I'm just sharing that the pace and the pressure of the profession sometimes (not often) leads to impulsive and not well-informed decisions.

By the next morning, the gates and the airspace re-opened and my patient was transported to the Burn Center in a stable condition and I was able to go home. As I was leaving, I found out that my friend's husband was still unaccounted for and she and her family were devastated along with hundreds of other families. That one day changed our world forever and changed how I would see my responsibility as a doctor.

In more ways than one, my experiences at Fort Hood really shaped my clinical practices and my commitment to the patients that I treat. Everyone knows that the military is a team-oriented profession and the saying, "you never leave a fallen solider behind" really resonated with me. I saw my patients as that fallen solider and I felt responsible to dig a little deeper in every case and look beyond the initial complaint. Pediatrics is an interesting field of medicine. In my mind, Pediatricians are like private investigators or behavioral profilers because when you think about it, most of our patients can't tell us what's wrong and even if they knew what was wrong they may not have the words to describe it. Instead, we rely on parents to deliver the story. This can be good and bad. Parents know their children best, but they also have an emotional attachment. They will come into the office in a panic telling you a story of their child who is lethargic and won't eat while you are looking at a child who is playing with everything in the exam room and eating from a bag of Cheerios. Where's the disconnect? Did the parent bring the wrong child to the appointment? No, not at all.

It's the parent's emotional attachment that makes them think the worst when their child isn't feeling well. And let's not forget the fact that kids are very resilient. They will actually heal themselves in the short ride to the doctor's office. Trust me, I have seen this more times than you can count. Now a lot of Pediatricians will take the clinical encounter at face value, if they see a well child then they will go with that and discount what the parent is saying. I, on the other hand, tend to value what a parent is saying but understand that sometimes the key information is not found in what the parent says but sometimes there is more value in what the parent has not said. This is where the investigation comes into play. I ask questions. . .I ask a lot of questions. In fact, I may go places in my questioning that parents haven't even thought to go. See also remember that often before a parent will come to my office for their child they have already visited the office of Google so many times they already have an answer or solution and they are just there for me to verify. For this reason, they don't always tell me the entire story but instead they tell me what Google said was important. I think you are starting to see how this can be problematic.

Now don't get me wrong, some things are very straight forward. In fact, there is a saying in Pediatrics that common things happen commonly. If it sounds like a cold, it probably is a cold. If you are describing dry, itching skin and the kid has a rash then it is probably eczema. This is not rocket science. However, what about the hyperactive child or the behavior problem. Ninety percent of the time, that child is going to behave themselves during the 15-minute doctor's appointment so should I say that there is no issue? I love it when parents will say things like, they have been told that a certain behavior is okay because their child is a boy or for a three-year-old this is just a prolonged case of the terrible twos. Huh?!? Don't ask me to explain either one of those statements because they don't make sense to me either. Just because you are a boy doesn't make it okay for you to throw chairs in your daycare class or to hit teachers and certain temper tantrums are not okay for even two-year old's, but they are called terrible twos for a reason. They aren't the terrible threes.

I believe statements like those are made because the parent's concern is challenging the Pediatrician outside of their comfort zone or what we like to call, our Scope of Practice. Sometimes the Pediatrician will think, this is not in my lane this is a problem for your teacher or you need to take this one to the behavioral specialist. To be honest, they wouldn't be wrong to think that way, but the parent brought their concern to you so tag, you're it!

Maybe you didn't realize this but in the healthcare profession you have a built-in team by design. For a child, the parent is the head of the healthcare team in my opinion and your child's Pediatrician is their Primary Care Manager whose job it is to handle all primary care issues and then to coordinate care when a specialist needs to be called in. So, if there is a problem that actually exceeds the scope of your Pediatrician that's when they mobilize their team to figure it out. That team may include the teacher and/or the behavioral health specialist depending on the issue at hand.

So here is where my frustrations started to build as a Pediatrician; I was finding that not everyone out there are team

players. I would have a child who was having behavioral problems and I would ask a lot of questions and figure out that
maybe there was an underlying reason for the behavior problems that we hadn't previously thought about. I would do my
part and evaluate for medical conditions like attention deficit
hyperactivity disorder (ADHD) and in doing so I might un-
cover other behavior issues that were outside of my scope. I
would attempt to activate team members by making referral to
Behavioral Health because I thought maybe there was a mood
issue like anxiety or depression and the referral would come
back and say, "yes, you were right they have ADHD". Or I
would ask them to go to the school for Cognitive Educational
Testing because ADHD and Learning Disabilities frequently
go together and would want them tested and the school would
assemble a meeting to say, "ADHD explains everything so there
is no reason to look at anything else". Over and over again, I
would place referrals and they would come back confirming
what I already knew without even looking for more. I was beginning to think that my team members weren't interested in
playing the game. I was getting frustrated and the parents were
getting frustrated. That fallen soldier was being left behind and
I was feeling powerless to do anything about it. I really felt like
I was missing something.

"I Turned Out Okay"

*It's always interesting when both parents come to the initial
appointment, especially when one is there reluctantly. Such was
the case with Kevin's parents. Kevin was a 9-year-old young man*

who was struggling at home and at school. Mom was concerned that there was something really wrong with Kevin and Dad had decided that he was just lazy. Sound familiar?

According to Kevin's mom he had always struggled in school. His grades were average, but Mom believed that he could do much better. Mom said several times that Kevin was very smart, but he just couldn't focus. Dad added that Kevin had absolutely no problem focusing on the video games that Mom continued to purchase for him and was able to focus to the point of not being able to tear himself away from the screen to complete his chores. Mom conceded and then added that Kevin had a difficult time completing homework and she often had to sit with him to make sure he got his work done. As hard as Kevin worked on his homework, more often than not he forgot to turn it in.

Kevin's teacher complained to his parents that he was easily distracted in class and needed constant reminders to stay on task. He frequently spoke out of turn and would often get in trouble for talking to his friends during quiet study time. Kevin frequently raised his hand to answer questions and when called upon would often add an off-topic comment. Most of the time, Kevin did not finish his classwork and would have to miss recess sometimes to complete his work. Previous teachers had mentioned ADHD to his parents during parent teacher conferences, but Dad didn't want to entertain the idea. He affirmed during the visit that he didn't believe Kevin had ADHD and felt he was very capable just not interested. Although Mom felt Kevin may have features of ADHD she feared the idea of medication, so she never pursued the diagnosis. Until now . . .

Kevin's grades were dropping and so was his self-esteem. He started asking to stay home from school complaining of a stomach ache or a headache. Last week, Kevin told his Mom that he was stupid and hated school. He said that he needed help. Mom requested a Student Support Team meeting at the school but was told that she would have to wait several months because their meeting dates were all full. Since the teacher had reported that Kevin's grades were average the team recommended that his teacher implement informal interventions and use this semester to monitor his response. Mom was not happy with the school's lack of support and decided to get a private evaluation.

By this time, Kevin's dad had grown impatient with the questions. He stated that he felt that this was all just a waste of time and he knew because he was just like Kevin growing up and he didn't have ADHD even though a teacher or two and a doctor had tried to convince his parents that he had it. Dad said that he didn't need any medication or special accommodations when he was in school and he turned out okay. All Kevin needed was a little discipline and Mom needed to stop babying him.

I decided to ask Dad a few more questions about his academic experiences growing up. I asked if he had ever missed recess because he had to complete assignments and Dad admitted that he had. When asked how he felt about it he said that he preferred to play with his friends, but he had to get his work completed. He said that his Mom worked with his teacher so that he could take his work home instead of missing recess. So, I asked whether he participated in any afterschool activities or sports. Kevin's dad stated that he never had time to do anything after school because it took so long to get his homework done that there wasn't even any time to play outside before it was too dark. I asked Dad what his goals were after high school graduation and he said he had wanted to go to college, but he didn't score high enough on the SAT to get accepted because he was so distracted by the other students taking the test that he didn't finish all of the questions before he ran out of time.

After Dad told his personal story, we all sat there in silence for a few minutes. Mom finally spoke up and said to Dad, "I don't want Kevin to sacrifice his childhood the way it sounds like you did. You think you turned out okay, but I'm not so sure."

If your child has diabetes or asthma, would you not want him to have medication or intervention? Why do we think of ADHD any differently?

CHAPTER 6:

What I Learned in Iraq . . . All Things Are Not Meant for All People

As military assignments go, I spent 3 years at Fort Hood before being reassigned to DeWitt Army Community Hospital at Fort Belvoir in Virginia. I was excited to move to Virginia because I would be closer to my extended family in Ohio and my older daughter would be in the same state as her father. I was also interested in starting fresh in a new clinic and working on building my team. In addition to being a staff Pediatrician I became the Chief of the Pediatric Service which put me in a much better position to network with providers in other clinical areas in support of our patients.

Not quite a year into my assignment I was again becoming frustrated in my efforts to coordinate care for my patients who had behavioral and academic issues. They were getting stuck in the same loop that my patients at Fort Hood were stuck in where they were being sent to me by the school because of an issue there, I would do what I could as far as evaluating for a medical condition and then I would refer them for testing or a behavioral health concern just for them to hit a wall. I was starting to think that this was not an issue with military medicine but maybe this was more pervasive and reflected a lack of understanding of the capabilities of the schools and the behavioral health system. This was becoming a personal priority for me not just because of my concern for my patients but more so due to my personal connection with learning issues and my need to help kids before they had to endure some of the challenges that I had experienced.

After determining that I had a learning disability in medical school, I had received formal accommodations during exams which included receiving extra time to take the exam and being allowed to test in a separate room from my peers. This was huge for me since I had always been a poor test taker and being accommodated in this way, allowed me to use strategies I had been taught to recall information and work through situations to determine the correct response. The last test that I had to take as a Pediatrician was the board exam. At the time, being board certified was not mandatory but it was expected that you obtain this certification as a testament to your skills and abilities as a Pediatrician. Also, at this time the boards were only offered once a year in October and I didn't register for the first opportunity to take them since I was transitioning back to the Army. I did register the following year but didn't have time to study because of the extra demands placed on me as a result of the war in Iraq. I failed my first attempt at the boards. To be completely honest, I think it was the fear of failure that impeded my study efforts much more than the extra demands placed upon me, but I convinced myself at the time that this was the story I was sticking with. I registered for the boards the following year and withdrew when I had gotten orders to move to Virginia. Once again, I convinced myself that I wouldn't have adequate time to study with the transition and I was also pregnant, so I was setting myself up for another failure. Once I was settled in Virginia I re-registered for the boards and this time I requested accommodations for my learning disability. I don't know why I hadn't done so in the past since I had received accommodations on the USMLE exams, but I felt like I didn't need the accommodations and could do this on my own. I was beginning to believe that if I couldn't pass the boards then that would mean that I wasn't a good doctor. It did not matter to me that all of my professional and clinical evaluations were stellar and my actual patients expressed satisfaction and never disappointment with our visits.

To make a long and painful story short, I was not granted accommodations for the board exam and was again determined to do this on my own. I had registered for a board review course (I think this was the third or fourth one that I attended) and I put myself on a strict study schedule. Midway through the year-long study process I received orders to deploy to Iraq for a year. These were not just any orders, I was being sent as an individual augmentee to join a National Guard unit in Ramadi as their Brigade Surgeon (medical advisor to the Infantry Brigade Commander) responsible for the Brigade's entire medical operation that was spread out across seven forward operating bases in the region. Oh, did I mention that I was told that I would be leaving in 7 days and the day I would leave (July 23, 2015) was one day before my younger daughter's first birthday. I don't even think I have to explain what I was feeling that day and that week; if you are human at all you get it. Luckily the pre-deployment station didn't have room for me on the 23rd so I was given an extra week to get myself and my family ready for my one-year absence. I packed my military equipment and my board review books and headed off to Iraq.

While I was in Iraq I studied harder than I ever had before in my life. I stuck to my strict schedule of getting up around 5 am, going to the gym to work out, I worked at least 8 hours every day and studied 2-3 hours every evening. I took several practice exams and knew more about pediatric medicine than I ever cared to know. The plan was that I would go home to take the exam in October and I would combine my board leave for one week with my two-week mid-tour leave. I was excited to get 3 weeks at home because my departure was so quick that I didn't get an opportunity to spend any time with my extended family before I left. By the time I was preparing to leave Iraq for the boards only my one week for the board exam had been approved. I had been given a ticket to return back to Iraq on the day following my test and was told that unless something changed my mid-tour leave would not be granted. I was upset beyond belief. My anxiety level grew, and I couldn't think or concentrate on my final exam preparation. When I arrived home, I was given the name and contact number of the person who was managing my leave paperwork and who would be able to tell me if my leave would be granted before my return flight. I had a study schedule for the first couple days home that went right out the window. My family was so excited about my being home that they could not care less about the fact that I was supposed to be studying. My kids just wanted to spend as much time with me as possible and how could I say no. I was stationed in Ramadi, which was the most dangerous part of Iraq during this time of the war and my family was in constant fear for my safety. How could I ignore their requests for time when I knew their fear was that they may not see me again. I went to a hotel the night before the boards so that I could get my mind right and focus on the task before me. The first day of the test went well but I was mentally exhausted when it ended 8 hours later. That evening I found it difficult to concentrate and sleep since my leave had still not been approved which meant I would be leaving early in the morning the day after my test. The second morning of the exam, I was tired, frustrated, anxious and distracted. I couldn't process and was overwhelmed by the other test takers who finished early. All I could think of was to finish this test as soon as possible so I could get one last evening with my family before I had to head back to the war zone. Unfortunately, that's exactly what I did. I finished my lunch and entered the last afternoon of the test. I didn't think I just colored the bubbles as fast as I could. I knew the test was important but given the situation it was not more important than the last 4 hours I would have with my kids before returning to Iraq. When the test was finished, and I was driving home, I received a call that my leave had been granted and I didn't have to return to Ramadi for two more weeks. I enjoyed those last two weeks, knowing in the back of my mind that I would have to take the most horrible test of my life again. I got that one right . . .

About a year later I made my last attempt at taking the boards. This time I hired a personal board exam coach. I attended another board review course and my personal coach customized my study plan so that I could stay on target. She determined my learning style and with that and her constant encouragement I thought I was ready. The third time was also not the charm and I failed again (not even close). My self-esteem was starting to take a serious hit. I was really beginning to think that I had chosen the wrong profession. I was successful clinically, my supervisors were happy, my patients were happy, and I was making a positive impact in my career. I was starting to doubt myself because I couldn't seem to pass this test even when I made it my priority and invested in resources that seemed to work for everybody else. I started to do some introspection and realized that no one had asked about my board certification status and the one or two times that someone did, they were not put off when they found out that I was not board certified. As a reflex I had registered for the upcoming exam but decided to withdraw. After much self-reflection I determined that all things are not for all people. I would like to be board certified but at what expense? The financial cost was not the real issue although I had spent well over $20,000 for all of my previous attempts to pass the test. The biggest cost was to my self-esteem and self-worth. I was a great doctor and my skills have been validated over and over by my patients and my colleagues. I am no longer willing to allow a test to stand in the way of my flourishing. . .Failure for me is not a testament to what I cannot do but an opportunity to reinforce what I can do and to refocus my efforts to recommit to my true purpose.

Adapt and Overcome

Bailey was an 11-year-old young man who was diagnosed with ADHD-combined type and autism level 2 after he was evaluated by our multi-disciplinary team. He initially came to the clinic with difficulty focusing and paying attention in school. He also showed frustration with transitions and some social isolation. His parents were very engaged in his care and were strong advocates for Bailey in school. He was started on a stimulant medication and his focus improved almost immediately. His grades improved. He started applied behavioral analysis (ABA) therapy to address functional and adaptive skills and through the supports offered on his individual education plan (IEP) in school he was allowed a sensory space in the school and worked with the Counselor and Occupational Therapist whenever he was overly upset.

Everything seemed to improve until Bailey started middle school. At this point, school caused him more stress than elementary school. He was having more emotional outbursts and would refuse to do assignments if they seemed either too hard or too easy. He was also struggling more in the home environment and was refusing to do everything to include chores, homework and even go places with the family. Everything had to be on Bailey's terms and he had to control all situations. The strategies that his parents had learned were not working and Mom's own frustration was building along with her anxiety. Bailey's mom had always had difficulty managing her own schedule and was known to be perpetually late. She lacked organization in her life and getting Bailey to all of his appointments was becoming more and more challenging especially with his constant refusals.

Bailey's 3-year-old sister was becoming more and more hyperactive. She was getting into everything and was starting to really get on Bailey's nerves. He was becoming more impulsive and his anger seemed to be directed towards his sister. Dad was less present in the home because of the need to increase the household income to cover daycare expenses for his daughter. Mom was becoming more and more overwhelmed. Things seemed to be working so well and now it appeared that everything was falling apart.

Mom brought Bailey to clinic for a medication follow-up appointment and it was obvious that she had lost control. Bailey was fine initially until his sister demanded that he give her his tablet. Of course, he didn't want to give it up and an argument ensued. Mom was attempting to answer questions about Bailey's response to the medication and she continued to get distracted by the kids and lost her train of thought on more than one occasion. She attempted to discipline the kids but was ineffective and their behavior continued to escalate. It was at that moment that Bailey's mom realized where Bailey's ADHD came from.

She realized that she would no longer be able to help Bailey and his sister until she first received help for herself. She had suffered for inattention, distractibility and impulsivity since for as long as she could remember but she thought she had learned how to compensate. She had never been evaluated or tested but deep down she knew she had ADHD. She figured that she had accomplished all that was important for her and her children needed to be her priority now, but she now knew that there was a reason for her to know if she had ADHD and maybe even to start medication herself. If she could be more focused and organized than she could help her children to be so as well.

Bailey's mom underwent evaluation, was diagnosed with ADHD, inattentive type and was started on a stimulant medication. She signed up to work with an ADHD Coach to help with organization skills and developed systems and routines to keep her children on task. The arguments stopped, and it seemed that her family was back on track. Sometimes you need to adapt the treatment plan to overcome the new obstacles before you.

CHAPTER 7

Closing in On
My Calling

Less than a year after returning from Iraq I had been told
by my Commander that I was selected to join a unit that
would be going back for a 15-month tour. I couldn't believe
it! It was the height of the war in both Iraq and Afghanistan,
so I wasn't surprised. The problem was that when I returned
after the first deployment, my then 2-year-old daughter didn't
recognize me. She was so young when I left that she became
very attached to her dad and it took her a couple of months to
realize that I was her mother. I couldn't go again so soon, I felt
it would create an irreparable void for my family. I had a tough
decision to make and this time I had to put my family first. I
decided to leave Active Duty and join the Army Reserves and
I was so fortunate to have been offered a position at Walter
Reed Army Medical Center as the Regional Medical Director
for the Exceptional Family Member Program. They say that

everything happens for a reason, and my reason was about to become clear.

The Exceptional Family Member Program (EFMP) is a mandatory Department of Defense program that ensures that special needs dependents of Service Members are cared for as they transition to new duty locations. This was an administrative position for me as well as my staff which consisted of a Licensed Clinical Social Worker, a Psychologist and an administrative assistant. We didn't have any clinical responsibilities but strongly desired to see patients to keep our clinical skills strong. Then the question became, what would we do that would support our program's specific patient population and allow us to work together as a team. We decided to look at the make-up of the conditions held by our beneficiary population. The number one diagnosis was asthma but that wasn't one that would benefit from my team's individual areas of expertise. The number two diagnosis was ADHD and the number five diagnosis was Developmental Delay. We all thought this was perfect because we each had an interest and experience in working with kids who struggled with ADHD and my long-term frustration had surrounded those complex ADHD cases that had co-morbid conditions like developmental delays or autism. Isn't it funny how it seems that everything will always seem to circle back? They say God works in mysterious ways and I was beginning to feel like the choices being made in my life were not mine to make.

For the next several months my team and I worked on what this clinic experience would look like. We were so fortunate to not have any significant restrictions placed on what we did or how we did it, especially since we were not considered clinical assets for the organization so anything that we offered would be considered a bonus for our beneficiaries. We began our work by partnering with the Department of Developmental Pediatrics as well as the Department of Behavioral Health to ensure that we had the resources and training necessary to provide the assistance that these individuals required. We even had a Behavioral Therapist from Fort Belvoir join our team to ensure we had the therapy support that our families would need. It was determined that our clinic would be a referral clinic for pediatricians and family practitioners who felt that their patient's ADHD exceeded their scope of practice, but they did not meet the level of care needed for a Developmental Pediatrician. So, in essence, our clinic would bridge the gap between primary care and specialty care and we would offer the essential continuum of care to include medical, behavioral health, cognitive testing and educational advocacy services. With the help and support of many individuals from primary care, behavioral health and developmental pediatrics; the ADHD Clinic at DeWitt Army Community Hospital and Walter Reed Army Medical Center was born.

One half day per week we were at each facility and supported the ADHD population. Our services became so sought after that we were accepting referrals from patients as far away as Fort Bragg, NC. The response was tremendous and with our coordination of care, military families were receiving the supports from schools that they had long desired but often seemed so far out of reach. What you may not realize is that military families face an even steeper uphill battle in trying to access educational supports than a family that is rooted in the community and it all surrounds the fact that military families are transient. If they are lucky they will be in a community for 3 years. If they arrive to the new school division without an individual education plan (IEP) or 504 plan of accommodation in place they will have to request one from the new school. Often times since their child's issues are not known to the school they will request some time to get to know the child and determine what problems they are experiencing. This often can take half of the school year. At that point, schools will often want to implement supports through informal programs to determine the child's response to intervention and they will often use this response to determine if a full assessment for formal accommodations are warranted. In some school divisions where their resources are limited, this assessment could then take a large part of another year. With military rotations being between 2-3 years some military children fall through the cracks and don't quite make it through the entire process before they have to transition to another duty location and start the process all over again. Through the efforts of the ADHD clinic we were able to expedite the assessment process and then with the assistance of our educational advocate we were able to assist families in working with their schools so that children that had educational needs that required an IEP or 504 plan could have one developed and implemented prior to the families next move. After 5 years of maintaining the ADHD clinic exclusively for military families I decided that it was time to consider sharing the concept outside of the military community. This was not an easy decision for me to make and in my reluctance to leave a position that I loved, God stepped in and made the decision for me.

I knew from concept of the clinic model that it was the wave of the future, but I had absolutely no experience as an entrepreneur. In fact, I had no experience working in the civilian world since my first position out of uniform was within a military treatment facility. As a physician one could argue that medicine is the same no matter what outfit you were wearing which is true, but they don't teach doctors how to be business people in medical school. It was my plan to eventually go back to school and get my Master of Business Administration in Healthcare Administration prior to venturing into my private practice. I had even looked into the different Executive MBA programs especially designed for doctors and I had selected the program that I felt would be the best fit for me. But before I could apply for the program and follow my plan, my work environment changed for the worse.

In the military system, positions of leadership tend to change every two years. Service Chiefs will come and go as they need for jobs of greater responsibility increase which was no different in the organization in which I worked. When I first accepted the position as the Regional Medical Director for EFMP, I served under my first Chief for a couple of months before he transitioned to another leadership position. My next Chief was amazing! He trusted my leadership and the skills and abilities of my team and he essentially gave me the autonomy to determine the direction of the program working closely with my senior advisors at the Surgeon General's Office. Under his leadership we all flourished—my staff and the dependents that we supported. Then it all changed with his departure.

The next Chief didn't seem to understand the program and she resented my leadership and the amount of control that I had over the program. For years it was my program and she wanted it to be hers. This didn't work for anybody, least of all the clients. I felt sabotaged as did my staff and before I even realized what was happening, a hostile work environment had developed. I was the most uncomfortable that I had ever been in my career and I felt that I was not effectively carrying out my mission. My physical trainer frequently says to me that he intentionally makes me unbalanced during my training because it is from being uncomfortable that you experience the most growth. I didn't realize that at the time, but God made me so uncomfortable in what I thought was my dream job, that I was willing to step out on faith and answer my calling.

Maximizing Potential

It doesn't happen as often as I think it should, but sometimes a parent will come in for an evaluation when they don't have any specific concerns. They are looking for information that they can use to give their children an advantage.

April's mom had learned of our clinic when she was seeking an assessment for her youngest son, Ryan. After completing Ryan's comprehensive assessment which included medical, behavioral health and cognitive testing his mom felt empowered to provide Ryan with all the support he needed to be successful, not just in school but in life. Her oldest child, April, was 13 and would be entering high school in the fall. April was a hard worker and an achiever. She spent many hours doing her homework, but Mom felt that it took her so long because she wasn't the most organized learner. She liked to do her homework in the kitchen because April liked to be around the family and she had to have her music playing in the background. April didn't like to read, and she always left her reading assignments to the end when Mom thought she was most tired. April was also a procrastinator and always waited until the last minute to start on large projects. The more Mom reminded her to get started the more frustrated and irritated April became. Despite all of April's faults, she still had an A/B average and was going to take at least one Honors level course next year.

April had a lot of friends, which was in direct contrast to her brother who struggled to make friends. April was always asked to birthday parties and events and it seemed that her social calendar was always full. Ryan had been diagnosed with ADHD and autism, but Mom just didn't see signs of either in April. She may have a little ADHD because she was disorganized and seemed to be distracted often but her grades were good, so Mom didn't think ADHD would need to be treated if she had it. What was most important to Mom was to understand April's potential. Mom wanted to have realistic expectations of April's abilities and didn't want to push her into honors and advanced placement classes if they would be a source of frustration for her.

April received a comprehensive evaluation for her attention, organization skills, cognitive abilities and mood. She was found to have a very high intellectual quotient (IQ) without signs of a learning disability. April does have mild attention deficit hyperactivity disorder, predominately inattentive type but as Mom had *suspect she did not require medication intervention. Because April's executive functioning skills (organizational skills) were weak, she was referred to an ADHD coach to work on strategies to improve her abilities to prioritize work and stay on task. April has strong self-esteem and didn't suffer from any mood related issues like anxiety or depression. What was interesting was that April's processing speed was slower than expected and her preferred learning style was musical analytical which means that she learns best when she fully understands the material and she needs background noise to concentrate. Based on this information, April's mom was encouraged to allow her to have some background noise in the room when she studies and to seriously entertain April's constant questioning of why something was the way that it was. Her mom was frequently frustrated by April's questioning of everything and had no idea that she genuinely had a desire to understand. Because Mom thought that April was intentionally being annoying she often responded to her questions of why by saying because I said so.*

Armed with the information from the evaluation, Mom went to April's school and requested a Student Support Team Meeting to discuss a 504 Plan of Accommodations for April's ADHD. Due to her slower processing time, easy distractibility and need for background noise; the school was willing to accommodate April with extra time on tests and projects, testing in a private room, tutoring time with her teachers to ask more questions about particular topics and permission to listen to a metronome on her cell phone using one ear bud during testing and some lectures.

Due to the improvement in her academic performance with the knowledge of her learning style and supportive accommodations for her inattention, April decided to take two honors classes in high school to challenge herself to her maximal potential.

CHAPTER 8:

Prepared for My Purpose . . . Making Sense of It All

I want to know who told doctors that they should open up private practices? For the record, doctors are not trained in running businesses. We are known to be the WORST business people ever so why is it even an option. I think doctors believe that if they are good at doctoring (is that a word?) that is the most important part and the business piece will fall in to place. WRONG!!! I'm here to tell you that when I opened my practice I was a doctor, I was not an entrepreneur. Five years later I am reluctantly becoming an entrepreneur because I have realized that if I don't learn quickly how to run my practice like a business I will be no good to anyone—myself, my family and my patients all included.

I would say that 90% of doctors choose this profession because they genuinely believe in helping people. We lead with our hearts. When you add passion and a calling to the mix you have all the ingredients for a remarkable service but if you put too much of any one of these ingredients you could have a colossal failure. My first year in practice I was busy, very busy because I was offering a service that no one else was offering. When people realized my practice was there they came. My staff and I were working tirelessly but we didn't seem to be making any money. I was depleting my savings, 401K and finally my kid's college fund and I just couldn't understand why. The second year, I realized that it wasn't good enough to just submit the billing to the insurance company, you had to make sure that the insurance company was paying. At the time I was working with a billing company that wrote off more than 50% of the charges because the insurance company requested additional information that the billing company never sent. In fact, they never even asked me for the documentation which I guess was their excuse for not sending the information. So, we figured that out, hired an internal billing specialist, and we continued to see patients, but we still weren't making any money. That year I learned about something called payor mix. What that means is that each insurance company determines what your services are worth, so you want to make sure you vary the number of patients that you see from each payor to make sure that your mix is profitable. I guess you can figure out that I was seeing a majority of patients from the insurance companies that determined my services were worth the least so again I was in the red. There were many days that I wanted to just close up shop and get a real job. In fact, I did get a real job the third year in practice because I figured I couldn't afford to pay myself anymore so in addition to working 50—60 hours per week in my practice I also worked 8 -10 hours per week for someone else. I think I currently have about 4 sources of income just to make ends meet for my family. Even though I wanted to close I couldn't. . .my passion and my calling have kept me going. In case you have never seen it before, this is what stepping out on faith looks like. So, let's stop talking about the money and let's talk about the passion.

One day I was speaking to one of the nursing interns that was working in my practice. We were talking about her future and she was saying that she didn't know exactly what she want- ed to do but she didn't think she enjoyed the program of study that she was currently involved in. She said that she knew she was getting good experience and was thankful for the opportu- nity, but she wasn't happy. I shared with her that I felt she was doing an amazing job and seemed to have a special knack for working with children with special needs. She really seemed to shine and excel when I watched her work. She stated that she felt trapped because her current financial situation as a single parent really didn't allow her to do anything different at this time. I thought about what she was saying, and I began to draw parallels to some of my early experiences. I often found myself doing things not because it was really what I wanted to do (remember West Point) but because it seemed like what I was meant to do at the time. What was interesting was that this was the first time everything started to come together for me. In that moment I was able to clearly see why I had been given all the opportunities and experiences that I had been given in my life and they were all intended to prepare me for that moment. I said to the nursing student that sometimes God will bring you to a place in your life that is uncomfortable and that doesn't make sense. You may even be unhappy or dissatisfied in that place but for some reason you will grow, prosper and excel in that position. That is in fact the key. If you can do well in spite of your negative emotional response then I believe you need to push through because there is a reason that you are in that place, with those people, having that experience and you are learning. It may not be clear in that moment but one day it will become clear and you will be grateful that you persevered.

I can now look back with a clearer understanding of why I have had almost every experience good and bad in my life and how they fit together. I remember when I turned 40 that I used to pray every night for God to show me my purpose. What would he have for me to do in this life. I felt I had accomplished most of what I had endeavored to do, and I believed that I would find pure joy in my life when I surrendered to fulfill his mission for my life. Money, stature and position were no longer important. So long as I could provide for my family and support my kids in their preparation for their goals and dreams then I would be satisfied.

I used to be embarrassed to say that I couldn't read when I was in second grade, I now embrace it because I feel that I can relate to my patients who present as a smart kid with inner turmoil. My ability to compensate is reminiscent of my patients who have learned to think outside the box. Like so many, I deferred my own gratification to follow an opportunity that my parents made for me. To this day, I will say out loud that if I had it to do all over again, that I would not go to West Point, but the reality is that many of my most memorable experiences have been possible because of the Army. Not only that but my daughter would not be a lawyer today (or would have twice as much debt) if it were not for the Post 9-11 GI Bill. My biggest failures and my responses to them, have had the greatest impact on who I have become. I have learned that failure doesn't mean you can't but instead it just means you have to find another way. With all my faking it to this point, my exposure to the special needs community afforded the right platform to bring it all together and finally make it.

I say on a daily basis that "Pediatric Partners for Attention and Learning is a multi-disciplinary clinic that bridges the gap between medical, behavioral health and cognitive educational services. We work with individuals from 18 months of age to adults to help them reach their fullest potential academically, socially and in life." I believe those words and they have become my words to live by. In every child, adolescent and adult I see myself or a member of my staff. I know that they are struggling now but with a little bit of love, support and faith that they will succeed. Parents come to the clinic looking for ways to "fix" their kids but the reality is that they are not broken so they don't need to be fixed. What they need is understanding . . . they need to understand themselves. Their strengths, their weaknesses and their motivations.

If an individual has ADHD, autism or a learning disability then they have a neurodevelopmental disorder. What that means is that they are born that way, it is who they are. I always find it interesting when a child comes to clinic and says that they can't focus. How do they know that? If you have never been able to focus, how do you know what it means to focus. They say the words because they have heard them used to represent them over and over, so they have adopted the term but if you don't know what it means to focus how are you going to be able to make yourself do it. So, the first step is always understanding.

I have spent many years preparing for this moment, for my time to make a difference in the lives of others and I'm taking it. No matter how hard it may get, my passion will not allow me to fail. I've stepped out on faith and my faith has prepared me to succeed.

Keeping the Faith

Destiny had a complex medical history starting with being premature and having some early developmental issues involving speech and motor activity. She was a tough kid though and despite her challenges she maintained a positive attitude and always had a smile on her face.

Destiny's mom requested a consultation to discuss her concerns with Destiny's academic performance. Destiny was 16 and hadn't done very well academically. She was approaching the end of her high school career and Mom was beginning to become concerned that she might not graduate. One of the problems was that Destiny was not concerned. She would fail a test or have a 20 average in a course and Destiny acted as though everything was fine. Mom felt that she seemed oblivious to everything and even though she studied and put forth effort it was like Destiny just didn't get it.

She had been on medication for her ADHD which had proven helpful for a time but last year Destiny requested to stop the medication. Destiny had an individual education plan at her previous school for ADHD and a processing disorder. For some reason, the IEP didn't transfer to the new school and she stopped receiving support. Her current school acted like she was doing her personal best and did not push her to do any better. Mom felt like the school had just given up and so did Destiny.

Destiny had an expectation to go to college, but Mom felt that was totally unrealistic. Typically, she was a C student and Mom questioned how she was ever going to graduate with F's in almost every class. She would do assignments and somehow, they never got turned in. She didn't finish class work or complete tests in class before the time ran out. Destiny response was to downgrade her goals from college to cosmetology school, but Mom feared that she would never leave home, live on her own or even take care of herself. Mom needed help and she needed someone to get through to Destiny and her school.

Destiny was evaluated by our team and found to have an average intellectual quotient (IQ), ADHD-combined type, specific learning disability in math and reading and autism level 2. She needed significant support services outside of school but just as importantly, she needed to re-establish an individualized education plan within the school. Mom and Destiny were thrilled to find that there was in fact more to the story than just ADHD and that there were targeted interventions to get Destiny back on track.

Destiny's mom hired an educational advocate to assist her in working with the school to determine the specific interventions needed to help Destiny improve her performance. Mom, with the advice of the advocate, met monthly with the school and Destiny also participated and was taught how to self-advocate and improve communications with her teachers. Over the course of the year Destiny improved her grades, established organized processes for tracking and completing her assignments, and gained a greater understanding of her learning challenges. At the end of that year, Destiny and her family moved to another school division in the southern part of the state. Destiny transitioned well into the new program and excelled in her program of study using the new learning strategies she had developed. By the middle of the year, Destiny had attained a straight A grade point average and had excelled on the college entrance exams. She refocused her goals, yet again and determined that not only did she want to go to college, but she believed that she could be successful as a psychology major.

The Best is Yet to Come . . .

So, where do we all go from here? This book is about action—a call to action. For you to realize that as a parent it is your responsibility to ensure that your child has every opportunity to succeed. Whether they are overtly struggling or just not performing to their potential. This book is also about you, the healthier you are as a parent the more available you will be for your children. Your time has not passed, it is right now.

I have been told over and over again that I needed to write a book. You can now see why I was hesitant. . .I was not born to write but I was born to be a change agent. To inspire others to step out on faith like I have done. What I realized is that I needed to share the stories, my story and those of my patients who have reached out for help. It is through these stories that others can see themselves and their children and find comfort in knowing that they are not alone and that understanding can be found.

I started writing this book a year ago and after the first two chapters I lost my inspiration and my motivation. I became bored, and since I personally don't like to read I convinced myself that no one else would want to hear my story either. I was recently mobilized by the Army Reserve to backfill for 4 months at Tripler Army Medical Center as a General Pediatrician. After my first couple patients, that frustration that I had lived with almost daily returned. I was again seeing patients who were struggling academically or socially, and their parents had stopped asking for help because they had already been caught in the loop between school—behavioral health and their provider. What made matters worse was that we are not training our primary care residents to recognize the subtle flags that patients wave as a cry for help. And when parents ask for help the providers aren't sure of their role or the roles of other key assessors and how they should all work together. Everyone seemed to want to help but no one had the tools to pull it all together. A multi-disciplinary, collaborative team that is coordinating care is the answer.

I realized during my time away from my practice that my job is far from done. I have found some of the answers, but I needed to share what I know and learn more to fill in the gaps that I don't know. I decided that this book was necessary but that was just the beginning. If I motivate someone by reading this book and then they don't know where to go for help, then I have contributed to another problem. I need to work with primary care providers, behavioral health professionals, school personnel and parents to educate them on this continuum of care. I need to help others to create multi-disciplinary teams and then show families how to access care. I need to lecture, host workshops and continue to write.

I know that sounds great for the future, but you may be asking yourself what can I do now and where do I go for help for myself or my child. If you are like most people, Google is your friend and that will be your first stop. Let me share a bit of caution, Google will provide anything you are looking for if you know what you want, if you don't sometimes it is not that helpful. I would recommend going to the national organizations that support what you may be concerned about. They will all provide detailed, research driven information about the conditions that they support as well as have local resources that can provide evaluation and treatment interventions in your area. A few of the resources that I use are below:

CHADD—The National Resource on ADHD
(www.chadd.org)
Autism Speaks (www.autismspeaks.org)
NADD—An association for persons with developmental disabilities and mental health needs (www.thenadd.org)

Additionally, if you are local to the Washington D.C., Maryland and Virginia area please check out the website for my clinic, Pediatric Partners for Attention and Learning, Inc. (www.PP4AL.com) or my personal speaking site, www.DrJoniMD.com. I would love to meet with you personally and my team and I would be honored to help you or your child reach your fullest potential. Lastly, download my app, Behavior Check, in the Apple App store or Android store to view my blogs, finds additional resources and even send me a personal question or concern that I will respond to via email.

I'm hoping that my best (and your best) is yet to come. . . stay tuned.

31801478R00057

Made in the USA
Lexington, KY
23 February 2019